Mark—The Gospel of God's Servant
Revised and Expanded

This is a self-study course designed to help you discover for yourself some important truths from the gospel of Mark.

how to study the lesson

1. Try to find a quiet spot free from distractions and noise.

2. Read each question carefully.

3. Look up the Scripture reference given after each question. Make sure you have found the correct Scripture passage. For example, sometimes you will find yourself looking up JOHN 1:1 instead of 1 JOHN 1:1.

4. Answer the question from the appropriate Bible passage. Write, in your own words, a phrase or sentence to answer the question. In questions that can be answered with a "yes" or "no" always give the reason for your answer . . . "Yes, because. . . ."

5. If possible, keep a dictionary handy in order to look up words you don't understand.

Copyright 1964, 1987 by THE MOODY BIBLE INSTITUTE OF CHICAGO
The author used the King James Version when preparing the questions for this manual.

ISBN 0-8024-5200-0
11 13 15 17 19 20 18 16 14 12
Printed in the United States of America

6. Pray for God's help. You *need* God's help in order to understand what you study in the Bible. PSALM 119:18 would be an appropriate verse for you to take to God in prayer.

7. *Class teachers using this course for group study will find some helpful suggestions on page 76.*

how to
take the self-check tests

Each lesson is concluded with a test designed to help you evaluate what you have learned.

1. Review the lesson carefully in the light of the self-check test questions.

2. If there are any questions in the self-check test you cannot answer, perhaps you have written into your lesson the wrong answer from your Bible. Go over your work carefully to make sure you have filled in the blanks correctly.

3. When you think you are ready to take the self-check test, do so without looking up the answers.

4. Check your answers to the self-check test carefully with the answer key given on page 77.

5. If you have any questions wrong, your answer key will tell you where to find the correct answer in your lesson. Go back and locate the right answers. Learn by your mistakes!

apply
what you have learned
to your own life

In this connection, read carefully JAMES 1:22-25. It is only as you apply your lessons to your own life that you will really grow in grace and increase in the knowledge of God.

[handwritten annotations at top: Jesus / worker, servant, miracles / written for gentiles not familiar with old testament / prophesies — Mark noted brevity + vividness]

Introduction to Mark

Mark is preeminently the gospel of service and presents the Lord Jesus Christ as the servant obedient unto death (see Phillipians 2:7-8). The servant character of the Lord Jesus is shown throughout the book and is clearly stated in 10:45. Particular emphasis is given to the miracles that the Lord Jesus performed, thus demonstrating His deity. Jesus is seen primarily as a Worker rather than as a Teacher.

Mark wrote primarily for the Gentiles who were not familiar with the Old Testament prophecies. Therefore, he used only a few Old Testament references (1:2-3; 14:27; 15:28). Mark is noted for its brevity and its vividness.

The author was a relative of Barnabas and a companion of Paul in his later ministry. The date of the gospel is somewhere between A.D. 57 and 63.

Outline of Mark

I. God's Servant Presented (chap. 1)

II. God's Servant Begins His Work (chaps. 2-3)

III. God's Servant Works Miracles (chaps. 4-5)

IV. God's Servant and the World (chap. 6)

V. God's Servant Heals and Teaches (chaps. 7-8)

VI. God's Servant Transfigured (chap. 9)

VII. God's Servant Moves Towards Jerusalem (chap. 10)

VIII. God's Servant Revealed as King (chaps. 11-12)

IX. God's Servant Foretells the Future (chap. 13)

X. God's Servant Refused (chap. 14)

XI. God's Servant Crucified (chap. 15)

XII. God's Servant Triumphant (chap. 16)

God's Servant Presented

MARK 1

Chapter 1 tells of His baptism and temptation.

1. What is the general theme of the book?

1:1 _____

2. Under what titles did John the Baptist present Jesus?

JOHN 1:29, 34 *The lamb of God the Son of God*

3. What prophecy concerning the Messiah and His forerunner had been recorded some five hundred years before?

MALACHI 3:1 _____

4. What was the purpose of John's coming?

1:2-3 *To prepare a way for the Lord.*

5. What was the clear-cut message that John gave?

1:4 *repentance for the forgiveness of sins*

6. What response did John's preaching bring from the people?

1:5 *Confessed their sins & baptized in Jordan*

7. What two actions are involved in true repentance?
conceal sin not prosper.
PROVERBS 28:13 *Confessed & renounce & find mercy*

8. Was there anything about the appearance of John that suggested earthly pomp?

1:6 _clothes of camel hair + leather belt_

9. What place did John take in relation to Christ?

1:7 _he will be powerful one._

10. Distinguish between John's baptism and Jesus' baptism.

1:8 _____

11. Where was Jesus baptized?

1:9 _____

12. What three things happened when Jesus came up out of the water?

1:10-11 _____

13. Did Jesus confess any sins when He was baptized?

2 CORINTHIANS 5:21 _____

14. Why did Jesus insist upon being baptized?

MATTHEW 3:14-15 _____

In His case, it was not baptism "unto repentance" but "unto righteousness." To John, this occurrence was a sign that Jesus was the promised Messiah. To Jesus Himself it was His identification with sinners, whom He had come to save.

15. What did the voice from heaven say?

1:11 _____

16. How is the Trinity seen in these verses?

1:10-11 _____

17. Where did Jesus go immediately after He was baptized?

1:12 _____

18. By whom was Jesus directed to go into the wilderness?

1:12 _____

19. How long did the conflict with Satan last?

1:13 _____

20. What gospel did Jesus preach?

1:14 _____

21. Explain the differences (if any) between the messages of John and of Jesus.

1:4, 15 _____

22. What is this kingdom called in Matthew's account?

MATTHEW 4:17 _____

23. Did Jesus call idle men to be His followers?

1:16 _____

24. Name the first disciples whom Jesus asked to follow Him.

1:16, 19 _____

25. What kind of fishermen did He intend to make of them?

1:17 _____

26. Were those men willing to give up a good business to follow Jesus?

1:18-20 _____

The call of Christ should be superior to either parental claims or the claims of a prosperous business.

27. What was there in Jesus' manner that astonished the people?

1:22 _____

28. How should God's Word be taught today?

1 PETER 4:11 _____

There is no real authority in Christian teaching that does not emphasize Christ as the Son of God and profound belief in His Word.

29. What shows that the personality of the man in the synagogue was under the dominion of a foreign spirit?

1:23-24 _____

30. What title did the demon give to Jesus?

1:24 _____

31. Is it possible that one could recognize Jesus as the Son of God and still not be saved?

JAMES 2:19; MARK 5:1-9 _____

32. What did Jesus say that showed the man's testimony had the devil behind it?

1:25 _____

33. Give the events of one day with the Lord.

1:21-34 _____

_____

34. What good example did Jesus set after a busy day?

1:35 _____

35. Did Jesus let the pressure of work interfere with prayer?

1:35 _____

36. Did the leper doubt the power of Jesus to heal, or His willingness?

1:40 _____

37. Should we put the "if" on Jesus or on ourselves?

9:23 _____

38. How did Jesus show that He was "moved with compassion" toward the leper?

1:41 _____

39. What shows that Jesus did not want to be advertised among men as a wonder-worker?

1:44 _____

40. How many verses in this chapter begin with the word *and*?

Chap. 1 _____

41. The word *immediately* appears how many times in this chapter?

Chap. 1 _____

42. What do we learn about the ministry of Jesus from questions 41 and 42?

_____

43. What impressed you about the ministry of Jesus in chapter 1?

_____

check-up time No. 1

You have just studied some important truths about the coming of the Lord Jesus. Review your study by rereading the questions and your written answers for lesson 1. If you aren't sure of an answer, reread the Scripture portion given to see if you can find the answer. Then take the following test to see how well you understand the important truths you have studied.

In the right-hand margin write "True" or "False" after each of the following statements.

1. The purpose of John's coming was to prepare the way for the Messiah. _____

2. John the Baptist presented Christ as the Good Shepherd. _____

3. Malachi gives a prophecy of the coming of John. _____

4. John considered himself to be greater than Jesus. _____

5. John said men must repent of their sins. _____

6. Jesus did have to confess sin. _____

7. Satan tried to keep the Lord Jesus from accomplishing His purpose in coming. _____

8. Jesus taught with authority because He is God. _____

9. Jesus' prayer life is an example to us. _____

10. Jesus worked miracles only to get the attention of the crowds. _____

Turn to page 77 and check your answers.

God's Servant Begins His Work

MARK 2 AND 3

Chapter 2 tells of the healing of the palsied man.

1. During this period of ministry, what city did Jesus seem to consider home?

2:1 _____

2. In this account whose faith did Jesus see?

2:4-5 _____

3. What did Jesus see beneath this man's physical troubles?

2:5 _____

4. Did Jesus always tie sickness to a person's sins?

JOHN 9:3 _____

5. Why did the scribes deny Jesus the right to forgive sins?

2:7 _____

6. What attribute of God does Jesus exhibit?

2:8 _____

7. Why did Jesus have the authority to forgive sins?

JOHN 14:7-11 _____

8. How did Jesus prove that He was able to forgive sins?

2:10-11 _____

9. How long did it take for Jesus to heal the man?

2:12 _____

10. Who got the credit for this miracle?

2:12 _____

11. What was the reaction of the people to this miracle?

2:12 _____

12. What type of response was Jesus getting from the people?

2:13 _____

13. What was Levi's name later changed to?

MATTHEW 9:9 _____

14. What was Levi's business?

2:14 _____

15. When the scribes and Pharisees had a complaint against Christ, to whom did they go?

2:16 _____

16. What was the complaint of the scribes and Pharisees against Jesus?

2:16 _____

17. Whom did Jesus come to call?

2:17 _____

18. Are there any who are not sinners?

ROMANS 3:23 _____

19. How often did the Pharisees usually fast?

LUKE 18:11-12 _____

20. Did Jesus believe fasting should be done regardless of circumstances?

2:19-20 _____

21. What would happen if a piece of unshrunken new cloth were sewed onto a piece of old cloth?

2:21 _____

22. What did Jesus mean by the parable of sewing a new piece of cloth on an old cloth?

2:21 _____

23. Did the disciples, according to the law, have the right to pluck corn on the Sabbath to satisfy hunger?

DEUTERONOMY 23:25 _____

24. Whom did Jesus use as an illustration to show that ceremonial observances must sometimes be set aside?

2:25-26 _____

25. Who had full authority over the Sabbath?

2:27-28 _____

26. What was the purpose of the Sabbath?

2:27 _____

Chapter 3 opens with the story of the man with the withered hand.

We may see in this incident a parable of service. We speak of one who does something skillfully as a "good hand." The hand is the organ for ministering, and when sin stops its usefulness it soon becomes paralyzed from inactivity.

27. Why did "they" watch the actions of Jesus?

3:2 _____

28. What was the first thing Jesus required of the man?

3:3 _____

29. Why does the Lord likewise demand that we stand out before men in confession of Him?

ROMANS 10:9-11 _____

Jesus has no silent partners. We must step out upon His Word without being ashamed of our position before men.

30. Is it ever right to refuse to do good on any day of the week?

JAMES 4:17 _____

31. What was seen in Jesus' expression?

3:5 _____

32. What caused Jesus to be grieved?

3:5 _____

Note that the only way to be angry and not sin is to be angry at nothing but sin.

33. What did Jesus tell the man to do?

3:5 _____

34. What was the result of this man's attempting the humanly impossible in obedience to Jesus' command?

3:5 _____

35. What two groups got together in their attempts to destroy Jesus?

3:6 _____

36. From what source was there an acknowledgment of the deity of Jesus?

3:11 _____

37. Did Jesus want such testimony to His deity?

3:12 _____

38. Where was Jesus when He called His disciples?

3:13 _____

39. What double purpose did Jesus have for them?

3:14 _____

40. What special authority was given to the disciples?

3:15 _____

41. What special detail is always given in connection with Judas?

3:19 _____

42. What name is always first among the disciples? What name is always last?

3:16-19 _____

43. Should one who follows Jesus expect to sometimes be misunderstood by his friends?

3:21 _____

44. How did the scribes say that Jesus did His miracles?

3:22 _____

45. Who was Beelzebul?

3:22 _____

46. Why was their argument senseless?

3:23-26 _____

47. What did Jesus say about the sin of attributing His works to the power of the devil?

3:29 _____

The sin that has no forgiveness is not a common sin. Even the atheists and infidels of today could scarcely come to the degree of guilt of those who actually witnessed the works of Christ and then attributed them to a vile spirit.

48. Does Jesus promise to forgive and save all those who come to Him?

JOHN 6:37 _____

49. What did the people notice that Jesus apparently took no notice of?

3:32 _____

50. Whom did Jesus speak of here as being His mother and His brethren?

3:34-35 _____

It is remarkable that in the two cases where the mother of Jesus figures in the story of His ministry, she appears in order to be reproved and to be placed, so far as relationship was concerned, on the same plane as all obedient servants of God.

51. Did Jesus' mother and brothers reject Him and His message?

ACTS 1:14 _____

check-up time No. 2

You have just studied some important truths about the beginning of the ministry of the Lord Jesus. Review your study by rereading the questions and your written answers for lesson 2. If you aren't sure of an answer, reread the Scripture portion given to see if you can find the answer. Then take the following test to see how well you understand the important truths you have studied.

In the right-hand margin write "True" or "False" after each of the following statements.

1. Jesus was impressed by the faith of the palsied man. _____

2. Forgiving the man's sins was more important than healing his body. _____

3. The physical healing was proof of Jesus' ability to forgive sins. _____

4. Jesus said fasting was of no value. _____

5. The Lord Jesus used Jonah as an illustration that the Sabbath was made for man. _____

6. There is such a thing as righteous anger. _____

7. The demons acknowledged that Jesus was God. _____

8. Judas is always identified as the traitor. _____

9. There is a sin that can never be forgiven. _____

10. Family relationships can keep one from doing God's will. _____

Turn to page 77 and check your answers.

17

God's Servant Works Miracles

MARK 4 AND 5

Chapter 4 gives the parable of the soils and records the miracle of the stilling of the storm.

1. At this time of His ministry what type of following did Jesus have?

4:1 _____

2. What does the seed represent?

4:14 _____

3. How soon after the seed is planted does Satan make his counterattack?

4:15 _____

4. In the next class of hearers, why did the seed die so quickly?

4:5-6 _____

5. What usually happens to those who mistake feelings for faith?

4:17 _____

Nothing shows more accurately how deeply a person has gone with God than afflictions and persecutions for the Word's sake.

6. Why didn't the seed sown on the third type of ground mature and bear fruit?

4:7 _____

7. What class of people did it represent?

4:18-19 _____

8. What three different degrees of fertility are noted in the fourth sowing?

4:8 _____

9. What does this mean?

4:20 _____

10. What was the purpose for sowing the seed?

4:8, 20 _____

11. What must be hidden from those who are not spiritually receptive?

4:11-12 _____

Parables are here shown to be necessary in dealing with the mixed crowd following Jesus at that time. He could not confide His full mind to them, but He could set them thinking by parables. The detailed explanations were reserved for those who were spiritually prepared to receive them.

12. What is the purpose of the light that has been given to us?

4:21 _____

13. If we respond to what we have heard, what will be the results?

4:24 _____

14. If we do not make good use of the knowledge we have, what will happen?

4:25 _____

Use or lose is a great principle.

15. If we plant gospel seed in true faith, what does God promise to do?

1 CORINTHIANS 3:6-7 _____

16. What happened at the close of the day after Jesus had given His disciples such wonderful teachings about faith?

4:35-38 _____

17. Had they really learned much about faith?

4:17, 38 _____

18. What is the relationship between fear and faith?

4:35-41 _____

19. Although Jesus had been sleeping the sleep of human exhaustion, what did He do that proved His deity?

4:39 _____

20. At what point did Jesus become the master of this situation?

4:35-41 _____

21. What other tumults is Jesus able to calm?

JOHN 14:27 _____

22. Did God always stop the storms for believers?

ACTS 27 _____

23. What fact about Jesus impressed His disciples now?

4:41 _____

24. What lessons do we learn about the storms in our lives from this passage?

_____

Chapter 5 tells of the healing of the demoniac and the woman, and the raising of Jairus's daughter.

There seemed to be a peculiar outbreak from the kingdom of darkness at the time of Christ's advent, as if the forces of evil had been held in reserve for that critical time, then to make their fiercest assault. Hence we read of the most remarkable instances of demon possession.

25. What was the cause of this man's superhuman strength?

5:2 _____

26. What effect did the sight of Jesus have upon him?

5:6 _____

27. How did he know who Jesus was?

JAMES 2:19 _____

28. What kind of tumult does Jesus here prove His power to calm?

5:8 _____

29. What habitation did the demons prefer to having none at all?

5:12 _____

30. How many pigs were drowned for the saving of a human soul?

5:13 _____

We need not feel sorry for the pigs, for they would have been butchered anyway. Perhaps the loss of the swine would remind the keeper that it was contrary to the law for Jews to keep swine. It served as an object lesson.

31. Did the people beseech Jesus to stay and heal their sick?

5:17 _____

32. What change is seen in the man's attitude toward Jesus?

5:18; cf. verse 7 _____

_____

33. What did Jesus ask the man to do?

5:19 _____

34. Why did Jesus have the healed man remain in the region of Decapolis?

5:20 _____

35. How was the woman's perfect faith in Christ revealed?

5:28 _____

36. How did Jesus discern this touch of true faith?

5:30 _____

The word *virtue* is used in the old medical sense. A physician speaks of the virtue of certain drugs, meaning their healing properties.

37. Why did Jesus ask who touched Him?

ROMANS 10:10 _____

38. What different results were received by the crowd and the woman?

5:21, 24, 27, 29 _____

39. After the messengers told Jairus of the death of his daughter, what did Jesus say to him?

5:36 _____

40. Although the child was dead as far as men were concerned, was she dead to Jesus?

5:39 _____

41. What is the difference in the crowd size at the two healings?

5:31, 37, 40 _____

42. Did the fact that the girl was miraculously healed do away with the necessity for human care?

5:43 _____

43. What shows that Jesus did not work the miracle in order to win the admiration of the curious?

5:43 _____

God's Servant and the World

MARK 6

Chapter 6 records the death of John the Baptist and the feeding of the five thousand.

1. What was Jesus' hometown? LUKE 4:16. _____

2. Why didn't the people of Nazareth accept the wonderful wisdom and works of Jesus?

6:2-3 _____

_____

3. From how big a family did Jesus come?

6:3 _____

4. If Jesus had worked miracles just to convince skeptics, where would He have done His mightiest works?

6:4-5 _____

5. What seemed to be the difference between the reception He received in Nazareth and that which He received from the villages surrounding that city?

6:3-6 _____

6. To whom were the twelve disciples sent at this time?

MATTHEW 10:5-6 _____

7. What instructions show that He wanted them to be devoted wholly to the preaching of the Word and to waste no time?

6:8-9 _____

8. Were they to allow themselves to be discouraged if their message was not received?

6:11 _____

9. What did they call upon men to do?

6:12 _____

10. Is there any indication that one disciple was more effective than the others in his mission?

6:7-13 _____   _____

11. Whom did Herod think Jesus was?

6:14 _____

12. What was Herod's attitude toward the gospel John preached?

6:20 _____

13. Why did Herod have a fear of John's return?

6:16-28 _____

14. Of the three—Herodias, her daughter, and Herod—which was the most responsible for the death of John the Baptist?

6:14-29 _____

15. How did Herod show that he was easily swayed by Herodias, the daughter, and others?

6:22-26 _____

16. How do we know that Jesus was interested in what the apostles accomplished on their mission?

6:30 _____

17. What was the greatest need of the multitudes who came to hear Christ?

6:34 _____

18. What did Jesus tell the disciples to do as a first step in feeding the people?

6:38 _____

We must not neglect the resources within our reach. If what we have is not working for God, it is of little use to ask Him to supply the needs. The workings of omnipotence are usually mingled with the gifts and labors of human hands.

19. What did Jesus do before distributing the food?

6:41 _____

20. Does Jesus want any of that which has been multiplied by His blessing to be wasted?

6:43 _____

21. If five loaves and two fish was sufficient for one boy, how many loaves and fish must Jesus have produced for the multitude?

6:44; MATTHEW 14:21 _____

22. What spiritual lesson did you learn from the feeding of the five thousand?

_____

23. What did Jesus always do after a great occasion?

6:46 _____

If Christian workers lack poise and power, it is because they do not pause for prayer and praise.

24. What happened as soon as Jesus stepped into the boat?

6:51 _____

25. What was the result in the disciples' hearts?

6:51-52 _____

_____

There can be no calm about us, no peace within us, and no progress for us until Jesus is aboard in our lives.

26. What should be our attitude toward the "storms" of life?

DANIEL 3:17-18; 2 CORINTHIANS 1:8-9 _____

_____

27. Even though Jesus had recently spent a long time teaching the people, what seemed to attract Him shortly afterwards?

6:56 _____

check-up time No. 3

You have just studied some important truths about the miracles of the Lord Jesus. Review your study by rereading the questions and your written answers for lessons 3 and 4. If you aren't sure of an answer, reread the Scripture portion given to see if you can find the answer. Then take the following test to see how well you understand the important truths you have studied.

Circle the letter beside the word that most accurately completes the sentence.

1. The seed represents (a) God, (b) people, (c) the Word.

2. The soils represent (a) actual ground, (b) different nationalities, (c) human hearts.

3. During the storm the disciples were (a) fearful, (b) trustful, (c) unconcerned.

4. Confession of Jesus' deity was made by (a) His disciples, (b) all the people, (c) demons.

5. After the healing of the demoniac, the people (a) begged Jesus to stay, (b) begged Jesus to leave, (c) were indifferent.

6. The healing of Jairus's daughter was (a) immediate, (b) gradual, (c) partial.

7. The twelve disciples were sent to preach to (a) Gentiles, (b) Jews, (c) everyone.

8. Jesus was unable to do miracles in Nazareth because of (a) unbelief, (b) disinterest, (c) persecution.

9. Herod thought Jesus was (a) a false prophet, (b) God, (c) John the Baptist.

10. Jesus went to a mountain apart (a) to get some rest, (b) to visit with the disciples, (c) to pray.

Turn to page 77 and check your answers.

God's Servant Heals and Teaches

MARK 7 AND 8

Chapter 7 records the rebuke of the Pharisees and the answer to the Gentile woman.

1. What two groups now find fault with Jesus?

7:1 _____

2. How important can traditions become to religious leaders? How far are they willing to travel to discuss them?

7:1 _____

3. Did they complain because the disciples did contrary to the law of God or contrary to tradition?

7:5 _____

The traditions were so-called inspired commentaries on the Old Testament law. The rabbis had added to the simple distinctions between clean and unclean food, endless rites and ceremonies.

4. Who had foretold the time when the chosen people would care more for the external form than for the reality of God's Word?

7:6 _____

5. What importance did the Pharisees and scribes give to the Word of God?

7:8-9, 13 _____

6. What example did Jesus use to show that these people gave more importance to tradition than to the Word of God?

7:10-12 _____

_____

7. In contrast to the emphasis on the traditions and the outward, where did Jesus put His emphasis?

7:6, 15, 21 _____

8. What is the first thing Jesus mentions as being the fruit of a corrupt heart?

7:21 _____

9. What is the source of all defilement?

7:23 _____

10. What can be done with such a heart?

PSALM 51:10 _____

11. How can we make sure that our hearts are right with God?

PROVERBS 4:23; PSALM 119:9, 11 _____

12. To be sure that we do not emphasize the negatives in our lives, what do we need to emphasize?

GALATIANS 5:22-23 _____

13. What seemingly harsh words did Jesus utter to the Gentile woman?

7:27 _____

_____

Note that the word for "dogs" is literally "little dogs" or "pet dogs," not the word often applied by Jews to Gentiles. Furthermore, much would depend upon the tone of Jesus' voice and the look in His eyes.

14. Who is the author of such faith as this woman showed?

HEBREWS 12:2 _____

Jesus was quickening and testing her faith. He knew that she would stand the test and have a purer faith than if she had received the blessing without a test.

15. How did the woman demonstrate that she had an unusual faith?

7:24-30 _____

16. What did the woman recognize about Jesus?

7:25-28 _____

17. What special commendation did she receive?

MATTHEW 15:28 _____

_____

18. How much contact with Jesus was needed for the daughter to be healed?

7:30 _____

19. Do you see any relationship between boldness and faith in this episode?

7:28-30 _____

20. What was the verdict of those who saw the miracle of the healing of the deaf and dumb man?

7:37 _____

Chapter 8 tells of the feeding of the four thousand and records Peter's confession of faith.

21. What proof is there that Jesus was concerned with the physical as well as the spiritual needs of the people?

8:2 _____

_____

22. Had the previous feeding of the multitude made much of an impression on the disciples?

8:4 _____

23. How does Jesus show that they had something that needed to be yielded to Him to be used?

8:5 _____

24. How much is Jesus able to supply in a desolate place?

8:8 _____

25. What was the motive of the Pharisees in seeking signs?

8:11 _____

26. How did Jesus show that He was not willing to spend His time on insignificant questions?

8:11-13 _____

27. What was the final sign Jesus gave?

MATTHEW 12:39-40 _____

28. What warning did Jesus give His disciples?

8:15 _____

The leaven of the Pharisees was formalism, and the leaven of Herod was worldliness.

29. What could the blind man see after Jesus first touched his eyes?

8:24 _____

30. What was the result of Jesus' second touch?

8:25 _____

There is a special lesson intended in the incident viewed in connection with what follows. Perhaps, also, there was a special reason in relation to the individual. Dr. Parker says: "Some men cannot stand instantaneousness."

31. Who were men saying Jesus was?

8:28 _____

Now we have an illustration of the gradual opening of spiritual eyes. The disciples did not have spiritual sight to see the deity of Christ all at once.

32. What was Peter's full answer?

MATTHEW 16:16 _____

Jesus made this utterance the cornerstone of His church. He saw in it the germ of all that living faith by which true believers should always be animated.

33. For what purpose was the Scripture given?

JOHN 20:31 _____

_____

34. When Jesus speaks of His death, what does He always connect with it?

8:31 _____

35. What seemed to be the reason for Jesus telling the apostles about His coming suffering?

8:31 _____

36. What part of the message had Peter not gotten for Jesus as well as for himself?

8:31; PHILIPPIANS 1:29 _____

37. To whom did Jesus attribute the suggestion that it was possible for Him to avoid the cross?

8:33 _____

38. What three elements belong to the one who decides that he wants to come after Jesus?

8:34 _____

39. In order to be a follower of Christ, what must one deny?

8:34 _____

40. What is implied in taking up His cross?

GALATIANS 6:14 _____

_____

To take up His cross means walking in fellowship with Him, involving one somewhat in the hostile treatment Jesus suffered.

41. Is all the pleasure of the world anything compared to the value of a soul?

8:36 _____

42. Why was Paul not ashamed of the gospel of Christ?

ROMANS 1:16 _____

43. What will be the price of being ashamed of Jesus and His words?

8:38 _____

44. Will one who is a true believer be ashamed?

ROMANS 10:11 _____

check-up time No. 4

You have just studied some important truths about the ministry of the Lord Jesus. Review your study by rereading the questions and your written answers for lesson 5. If you aren't sure of an answer, reread the Scripture portion given to see if you can find the answer. Then take the following test to see how well you understand the important truths you have studied.

Circle the letter beside the word that most accurately completes the sentence.

1. The Pharisees were most concerned with keeping (a) God's Word, (b) Roman law, (c) their traditions.

2. In God's sight evil thoughts are (a) not as bad as murder, (b) worse than murder, (c) as sinful as murder.

3. When Jesus saw the hungry multitude, He (a) provided food for them, (b) sent them away, (c) told the disciples to feed them.

4. As a final sign Jesus used the experience of (a) Noah, (b) Jonah, (c) Daniel.

5. Teaching about the death of the Lord Jesus is always connected with (a) His resurrection, (b) the cross, (c) Judas.

6. The disciple who confessed that Jesus was God's Son was (a) James, (b) Peter, (c) John.

7. The Scripture was given primarily that we may (a) be wise, (b) live a good life, (c) know how to be saved.

8. In Romans Paul speaks of the gospel as being (a) interesting, (b) powerful, (c) profitable.

9. Jesus will be ashamed of those who (a) follow Him, (b) turn away from Him, (c) are ashamed of Him.

10. To follow Jesus one must deny (a) money, (b) family, (c) oneself.

Turn to page 77 and check your answers.

God's Servant Transfigured

MARK 9

Chapter 9 tells of the transfiguration of Jesus and of the powerlessness of the disciples.

The transfiguration shows that the death Jesus had foretold was not the result of weakness on His part but the great purpose for which He had become incarnate. The word means a "complete and remarkable change," not merely outward, but substantial inward change as well.

1. Who were the "some" who had the opportunity of seeing His kingdom come in power?

9:2 _____

2. What could be the fulfillment of the glimpse of the kingdom of God in power?

9:1-8 _____

3. What is the connection between glory and suffering?

9:2-3, 12; 1 PETER 5:10 _____

4. When were the same three with Him again?

14:32-33 _____

What they saw and heard on the mount should have helped them to understand what took place later in Gethsemane.

5. Who appeared with Jesus?

9:4 _____

6. What did they talk about?

LUKE 9:30-31 _____

7. What rash proposal did Peter make?

9:5 _____

8. What were God's last words from heaven concerning His Son?

9:7 _____

9. How do we know that all this made a deep impression on Peter's mind?

2 PETER 1:17-18 _____

_____

10. How long were they to withhold the story of what had happened?

9:9 _____

11. What question troubled the disciples?

9:11 _____

_____

12. Who had already come in the spirit and power of Elias?

LUKE 1:13-17 _____

13. What was the cause of the excitement at the foot of the mount?

9:17-18 _____

14. What word suggested the father's doubt?

9:22 _____

15. Where did Jesus put the "if"?

9:23 _____

16. What response did the father make?

9:24 _____

17. What did Jesus say was the reason for the disciples' lack of power?

9:29 _____

_____

18. What spiritual lessons did the disciples learn as a result of asking questions?

9:28-29 _____

19. What was the reaction of the disciples when Jesus told them what was going to happen to Him?

9:31-32 _____

20. Was the resurrection a new subject to the Jewish disciples?

JOB 19:25; PSALM 16:10-11; 49:14-15; DANIEL 12:3 _____

21. How many times did Jesus tell His disciples that He was going to suffer?

8:31; 9:12, 31; 10:33-34 _____

22. What did Jesus say one must do in order to be first?

9:35 _____

23. Why did Jesus use a child as an example of His teaching on being a servant?

9:36-37 _____

24. How do we know that John had not learned the lesson of recognizing the value of other people's service for God?

9:38 _____

25. How does the value of performing miracles compare to giving cups of cold water in the sight of God?

9:38-41 _____

26. In order to receive a reward, how must one's service be done?

9:41 _____

27. What point was Jesus trying to make to John in responding to his statement?

9:38-41 _____

28. What does Jesus teach regarding people who live for themselves alone?

10:42 _____

29. What change is obvious in the emphasis of Jesus' teaching in this chapter compared to previous chapters?

9:12, 29, 31, 35, 41 _____

30. Was Jesus here teaching literal multilation of the body?

9:43-45; GALATIANS 5:24 _____

_____

It is better to part with anything or everything than to go to hell where conscience preys as a worm upon the soul, and where unsatisfied passions burn on forever (LUKE 16:24-25).

31. Does Jesus indicate that future punishment will sometime end?

9:48 _____

32. What do you feel is the emphasis of 9:42-50? Is it the awfulness of hell or the awfulness of causing people to stumble?

_____

33. What means does God sometimes use to perfect His children?

1 PETER 4:12-14 _____

34. What gives relish to everything in a Christian's life?

COLOSSIANS 4:6 _____

Insipid salt is another name for a savorless life. The grace of Christ communicates seasoning to a life that makes it different from any other life. The world despises a savorless Christian.

God's Servant Moves Toward Jerusalem

MARK 10

Chapter 10 tells of the rich young ruler, the dispute of the disciples, and the healing of Bartimaeus.

1. What seemed to be one of the main emphases in the ministry of Jesus on earth?

10:1c _____

2. What question did Jesus give in reply to the Pharisees when they asked Him about divorce?

10:2-3 _____

3. What word suggests that God tolerated divorce because of the sinful condition of men?

10:4-5 _____

4. Does divorce originate with God?

10:5-8 _____

5. What is God's basic plan for marriage?

10:6-8 _____

6. How close does God regard the union of husband and wife to be?

10:8 _____

7. Whom did Jesus rebuke for not permitting people to bring the children to Him?

10:14 _____

8. Is it a serious thing for anyone to keep a child from coming to Christ?

10:14-15 _____

9. What words indicate this?

10:14 _____

10. How important is touching to people?

3:10; 5:28; 6:56; 8:22; 10:13 _____

11. How did Jesus show His concern for children?

10:16 _____

12. Was there any possibility that the rich young man had perfectly kept the law?

JAMES 2:10-11 _____

13. What is the law intended to do?

ROMANS 3:19-20; GALATIANS 3:24 _____

_____

14. Was Jesus denying His deity in saying that absolute goodness is found only in God?

JOHN 10:30 _____

15. Is there any indication that the man recognized Jesus as the Son of God?

10:17-22 _____

16. Give the reason that Jesus did not refer to all the commandments.

10:19-22 _____

17. What action of Jesus shows that He recognized the young man's sincerity?

10:21 _____

18. Which of the commandments had the man not kept?

10:22; LEVITICUS 19:18 _____

19. No person is beyond God's ability to save but what is impossible for God?

HEBREWS 6:18; EXODUS 20:1-17 _____

20. What is the real danger of being rich?

10:24 _____

21. Who alone can work the miracle of making a rich man "poor in spirit" so that he will want to be saved?

10:27 _____

22. What are the rewards for following God completely?

10:28-31 _____

23. Are all our rewards future?

10:29-30 _____

24. What was going to happen to Jesus in Jerusalem?

10:33 _____

25. What statement of Jesus should have reassured the disciples that He was not going to be simply the victim of circumstances?

10:34 _____

26. What did James and John want for themselves?

10:37 _____

27. Who was the first martyr among the twelve?

ACTS 12:1-2 _____

28. What is the way of attaining heaven's highest honors?

10:44 _____

29. What was the first object of Christ's earthly life?

10:45 _____

_____

30. To which attribute of God did blind Bartimaeus appeal?

10:47-48 _____

31. Although there were multitudes of people, how did Jesus show that He is interested in individuals?

10:46-49 _____

32. What action of Bartimaeus shows his zeal to get to Jesus?

10:50 _____

check-up time No. 5

You have just studied some important truths about the Lord Jesus. Review your study by rereading the questions and your written answers for lessons 6 and 7. If you aren't sure of an answer, reread the Scripture portion given to see if you can find the answer. Then take the following test to see how well you understand the important truths you have studied.

In the right-hand margin write "True" or "False" after each of the following statements.

1. Peter, James, and John saw the transfiguration of the Lord Jesus. _____

2. The disciples failed to recognize the two men who appeared and talked with Jesus. _____

3. Peter soon forgot this experience. _____

4. Jesus was referring to John the Baptist when He spoke of Elias. _____

5. Children are important in God's sight. _____

6. The rich young ruler was just a hypocrite. _____

7. Jesus taught that only rich persons could be saved. _____

8. The disciples failed to understand when Jesus told them of His death. _____

9. Peter was the first of the disciples to die for Christ. _____

10. Bartimaeus wasn't sure Jesus could heal him. _____

Turn to page 77 and check your answers.

God's Servant Revealed as King

MARK 11 AND 12

Chapter 11 gives details of the triumphal entry.

We have here the account of how Christ planned the lowliest of all memorable parades. The very style in which Jesus made this entry should have proved to every reflective spectator that He had no intention at that time of acting the part of an earthly monarch.

1. Why should the people have recognized the manner in which Jesus entered Jerusalem?

ZECHARIAH 9:9 _____

2. On what will Jesus ride when He returns as King?

REVELATION 19:11 _____

3. What was unusual about the colt on which Jesus rode into the city?

11:2 _____

4. Why were the owners of the colt willing to let it go?

11:3-6 _____

5. What was done to the colt before Jesus sat upon it?

11:7 _____

47

6. What type of welcome did Jesus receive upon His entry?

11:8-10 _____

7. Why did the people cry out?

11:9 _____

_____

8. What kingdom did the people think was about to be set up?

11:10 _____

9. Should they have expected an earthly kingdom at this time?

ZECHARIAH 9:9 _____

10. What suggested that there should have been fruit on the fig tree?

11:13 _____

The figs usually appear before the leaves, hence, although it was not the time for either fruit or foliage, expectations would be raised on seeing the green leaves. This was a freak tree, an illustration of those who make great religious profession in season and out of season, and yet are without fruit. Jesus' many miracles were miracles of mercy. A useless tree is the only thing cursed.

11. For what is God's house to be noted?

11:17 _____

12. Give the reason for the cleansing of the Temple.

11:17 _____

13. How did the Jewish leaders respond to the cleansing of the Temple?

11:18 _____

48

14. How complete was the miracle upon the fig tree?

11:20 _____

15. What lesson did Jesus immediately suggest?

11:22-23 _____

_____

16. Is it possible for any Christian to bear fruit apart from faith? Explain.

HEBREWS 11:6 _____

17. Who is the author of true faith?

HEBREWS 12:2 _____

18. How are we to develop our faith?

ROMANS 10:17 _____

19. Why were the scribes and Pharisees unable to answer the question Jesus asked?

11:29-33 _____

Chapter 12 deals with the parable of the vineyard and the question of the resurrection.

20. Why would the Jews so well understand the parable of the vineyard?

ISAIAH 5:1-7 _____

_____

This parable is an Old Testament theme that is almost exactly repeated in Jesus' discourse.

21. What did Israel do to the prophets whom God sent to demand fruit?

MATTHEW 23:29-32 _____

22. What happened in "the fullness of time"?

GALATIANS 4:4 _____

23. What will be the fate of those who reject the heir?

12:9 _____

24. Who later made use of the Scripture that Jesus quotes from Psalm 118?

ACTS 4:10-11; 1 PETER 2:7 _____

The psalmist is said to have referred to an actual incident in the rebuilding of the Temple. A stone which the builders had rejected proved to be of such excellent quality that it was used for the cornice. The Jews had always understood this as referring to their Messiah.

25. Why were the Jewish leaders seeking to seize Jesus after He told the parable of the vineyard?

12:12 _____

26. What was the next catch question that was asked?

12:14 _____

27. What did Jesus' answer indicate about tax money?

12:17 _____

28. What unexpected response took place in the Pharisees and Herodians as a result of their questioning Jesus?

12:17 _____

29. How did Jesus show that we have a dual responsibility?

12:17 _____

30. What was one of the basic beliefs of the Sadducees?

12:18 _____

31. What example did the Sadducees give in an attempt to make the doctrine of the resurrection look ridiculous?

12:20-23 _____

_____

32. How did Jesus look upon this question?

12:24 _____

33. What was the reason the Sadducees were not able to answer the question they themselves asked?

12:24 _____

34. How did God refer to Himself in their own Scriptures?

12:26-27 _____

35. What was the sincere question of the scribe?

12:28 _____

The Rabbis counted 613 precepts, divided into "weighty" and "light." There were 248 affirmative and 365 negative laws. It was argued that of such a number, all could not be of the same value.

36. What infallible answer did Jesus deliver in one sentence?

12:30 _____

_____

37. What law did Jesus name as second in importance?

12:31 _____

38. In what way was this scribe different than the other scribes who asked Jesus questions?

12:28-34 _____

39. Why did the Jews cease asking Jesus questions?

12:34 _____

40. How was the multitude of people responding to the answers Jesus gave to the questions?

12:37 _____

41. How could the Christ David referred to be Lord and at the same time be the son of David?

12:35-37 _____

42. Against whom did Jesus then warn the people?

12:38-40 _____

43. Give the reason Jesus said that we need to beware of the scribes who live for public attention.

12:38-40 _____

44. Why did the widow's small gift make a greater impression on Jesus than any other?

12:44 _____

45. What is our standard of giving today, according to Paul?

2 CORINTHIANS 9:7 _____

God's Servant Foretells the Future

MARK 13

Chapter 13 gives the Olivet discourse.

1. What impressed the disciples as they were leaving the Temple?

13:1 _____

2. What seemingly improbable prophecy did Jesus make?

13:2 _____

Our Lord's prediction is more remarkable when it is known that there were stones of white marble sixty-seven feet long, seven feet high and nine feet wide. Josephus tells us that Titus held a council of generals and decided to save the Temple as an ornament to the Empire, but for some reason the soldiers disregarded. One greater than Titus had decreed that it should come down.

3. To whom did Jesus describe the events of the future?

13:3 _____

4. What were the two questions asked by the disciples?

13:4 _____

5. What was the opening warning of the prophetic discourse?

13:5 _____

6. What would characterize the entire age?

13:7 _____

7. What would happen to followers of Christ when war came?

13:9 _____

8. Give one comfort that the believer can have in the midst of suffering?

13:11 _____

9. What type of family relationship can we expect?

13:12 _____

10. What will be the signal that the believers need to flee from Jerusalem?

13:14 _____

11. List the restraints that are given to the believers.

13:15-16 _____

12. What did Daniel prophesy would take place after the cutting off of the Messiah?

DANIEL 9:26 _____

13. When was the desolation of the Temple accomplished?

LUKE 21:20-21 _____

Josephus tells us that the Romans brought their standards into the Temple and offered sacrifices to them. Bear in mind that there is a double fulfillment of these things, for the prophecies show a future gathering of armies about Jerusalem under antichrist.

14. What will happen at the close of the Great Tribulation described here, which Matthew's account shows is future?

MATTHEW 24:29-30 _____

15. What should a Christian remember when he hears reports of miracle workers and Messiahs?

13:21-23 _____

16. What evidence shows that the false prophet who says he is the Christ is not the Christ?

13:21 _____

17. How can the believer prepare for the end times?

13:23 _____

_____

18. Will the second coming of Christ be an historical event as His first coming was?

13:26 _____

19. What will happen in connection with His coming?

13:27 _____

20. What symbol in addition to the fig tree did Jesus use in speaking of Israel?

12:1 _____

21. What is the significance of Israel's gathering together after her long dispersion?

13:29 _____

22. What lesson can be learned from the fig tree?

13:28-29 _____

_____

23. In the midst of all this trouble, of what can we be confident?

13:31 _____

24. Who alone knows the exact time of the second coming?

13:32 _____

25. What is the responsibility of every believer?

13:34 _____

26. In the midst of this description of the trouble ahead, what commands are given to the believer?

13:9, 23, 33, 35, 37 _____

27. What is to be our chief concern while we wait for His return?

13:35-37 _____

check-up time No. 6

You have just studied some important truths about Jesus' teaching. Review your study by rereading the questions and your answers for lessons 8 and 9. If you aren't sure of an answer, reread the Scripture portion given to see if you can find the answer. Then take the following test to see how well you understand the important truths you have studied.

In the right-hand margin write "True" or "False" after each of the following statements.

1. Jesus' entry into Jerusalem was proof that He was planning to set up an earthly kingdom immediately. _____

2. Nobody noticed Him entering the city. _____

3. God's house is to be a house of prayer. _____

4. The nation of Israel was compared to the fig tree. _____

5. The Sadducees believed in the resurrection. _____

6. The most important commandment is to love God. _____

7. Daniel had foretold the destruction of the Temple. _____

8. The regathering of Israel as a nation is of great importance. _____

9. We can be sure that Christ will return. _____

10. It matters greatly what we do during His absence. _____

Turn to page 77 and check your answers.

God's Servant Refused

MARK 14

Chapter 14 tells of Jesus' agony in the Garden and of His arrest.

1. Who was the woman who anointed Jesus at this time?

JOHN 12:2-3 _____

2. Who first suggested the wastefulness of this act?

JOHN 12:4-5 _____

3. For what purpose did Jesus say the ointment had been given?

14:7-8 _____

4. What memorial was erected to this woman's gift?

14:9 _____

_____

This was a bold thing for one to promise, and yet the word of Jesus has been fulfilled for these 1,900 years. Only He who was the eternal Son could pledge the immortality of this woman's act.

5. How did Judas respond to the declaration of Jesus in 14:9?

14:10-11 _____

6. How much money was Judas willing to take to betray Jesus?

MATTHEW 26:15 _____

7. What did Jesus tell His disciples to prepare?

14:12-16 _____

8. What signals were to be used to indicate where the Last Supper was to be prepared?

14:13-16 _____

9. What strange utterance of Jesus disturbed the disciples as they ate?

14:18 _____

10. What did they ask Him?

MATTHEW 26:22 _____

11. Did the disciples suspect who was to betray Jesus?

14:18-19 _____

12. What happened to the man who did betray Jesus?

MATTHEW 27:5; ACTS 1:18-19 _____

13. Does Jesus indicate that there would be hope for Judas's salvation sometime in the future?

14:21 _____

14. What do the wine and the bread symbolize?

1 CORINTHIANS 11:24-26 _____

15. When will Jesus join the celebration of the Last Supper again?

14:25 _____

16. What did Jesus say would be the attitude of the disciples that night?

14:27 _____

17. Who insisted that he would always remain true?

14:29 _____

18. Did Peter and the other disciples believe that all the sheep would be scattered?

14:29-31 _____

19. What did Jesus predict about Peter's behavior?

14:30 _____

20. Who were with Jesus in the Garden?

14:33 _____

21. What were Jesus emotions as He entered into the Garden of Gethsemane?

14:33-34 _____

22. What did Jesus pray?

14:36 _____

_____

23. Although Jesus was God, how did He show His human feelings?

14:36, 39 _____

24. What shows the great agony of spirit Jesus was enduring?

LUKE 22:44 _____

25. What were the disciples doing during this time?

14:37 _____

26. Did they need to pray for Jesus or for themselves?

14:38 _____

27. How did Jesus show that He was still in control of the situation?

14:42 _____

28. Whom did Judas bring with him to arrest Jesus?

14:43 _____

29. By what title did Judas address Jesus?

14:45 _____

30. How did Jesus rebuke the religious leaders?

14:48-49 _____

31. Who left Jesus and fled?

14:50 _____

32. Does the account of the young man slipping out of the linen cloth have any bearing on the story?

14:51-52 _____

Tradition says that it was Mark, then a young man. Like many other small details in the account, it shows that the story is drawn from real life. We can understand how Mark, when writing this part of the story, would recall such a detail.

33. Who were the chief characters at the trial of Jesus?

14:53, 55 _____

_____

34. Where was Peter at this point of the story?

14:54 _____

35. What was the problem with the testimonies against Jesus?

14:56-59 _____

36. Did Jesus answer the false charges against Him?

14:60-61 _____

37. Did He reply when they questioned His deity?

14:61-62 _____

38. What type of treatment did they give to Jesus?

14:65 _____

39. How did Peter begin to fulfill Christ's words to him?

14:68 _____

40. What jarred Peter into the reality of his denial?

14:72 _____

41. Why was there such a difference between Peter and Judas in this matter?

14:72; MATTHEW 27:5 _____

42. In your opinion, what was the reason that Peter denied knowing Jesus?

_____

God's Servant Crucified

MARK 15

Chapter 15 tells of the death and burial of the Lord Jesus.

1. Who met as a council to make a decision about Jesus?

15:1 _____

2. What reason did the Jews have to bring Jesus to Pilate for judgment?

JOHN 18:31 _____

3. What did Pilate ask Jesus?

15:2 _____

4. Did Jesus deny that He was the "king of the Jews"?

15:2 _____

5. What was the response by Jesus to the accusations?

15:3-5 _____

6. What was the custom in honor of the Jewish feast?

15:6 _____

7. Who suggested that Barabbas, the noted criminal, be released?

15:11 _____

8. What crimes had Barabbas committed?

15:7 _____

9. Why was the request for the release of Barabbas rather than of Jesus?

15:9-10 _____

10. Could the religious leaders answer Pilate's question?

15:14 _____

11. Why did Pilate release Barabbas rather than Jesus?

15:15 _____

12. How did the soldiers mock the Lord Jesus?

15:17-19 _____

_____

13. Who helped carry the cross?

15:21 _____

14. What does "Golgotha" mean?

15:22 _____

15. Why didn't Jesus accept the drink offered to Him?

15:23 _____

16. What was significant about the soldiers' actions in verse 24?

PSALM 22:18 _____

_____

17. How did the inscription recorded by Mark differ from that recorded in the other gospels?

MATTHEW 27:37; MARK 15:26; LUKE 23:28; JOHN 19:19 _____

_____

18. Why was Jesus crucified between two thieves?

15:27-28; ISAIAH 53:12 _____

19. In what way did the passers-by and the chief priests mock Jesus?

15:29-31 _____

20. At what hour was Jesus nailed to the cross?

15:25 _____

21. What happened between the sixth and ninth hours?

15:33 _____

22. At what hour did He die?

15:34 _____

23. Could Jesus have saved Himself and sinners at the same time?

15:31 _____

24. What agony climaxed the awful sufferings of Jesus?

15:34 _____

25. Why did God the Father turn from the Lord Jesus?

HABAKKUK 1:13; 2 CORINTHIANS 5:21 _____

_____

26. What victorious shout did Christ give?

JOHN 19:30 _____

27. Why did Jesus die?

15:37; 1 CORINTHIANS 15:3 _____

28. Who took Jesus' life from Him?

JOHN 10:18 _____

29. What was the significance of the rent veil?

HEBREWS 9:6-8; 10:19-20 _____

_____

30. What opinion did the centurion have of Jesus?

15:39 _____

31. What place did the women have in the life of Jesus?

15:40-41 _____

32. Who asked for the body of Jesus?

15:43 _____

33. What place of prominence did Joseph of Arimathea hold?

15:43 _____

34. What did Joseph do with the body of Jesus?

15:46 _____

35. Who waited to the end to see where the body of Jesus was laid?

15:47 _____

check-up time No. 7

You have just studied some important truths about Jesus' death. Review your study by rereading the questions and your written answers in lessons 10 and 11. If you aren't sure of an answer, reread the Scripture portion given to see if you can find the answer. Then take the following test to see how well you understand the important truths you have studied.

Circle the letter beside the word or words that most accurately complete the sentence.

1. The woman who anointed Jesus was (a) Mary, His mother, (b) Mary Magdalene, (c) Mary of Bethany.

2. Jesus said He would be betrayed by (a) one of His disciples, (b) the people, (c) the Pharisees.

3. The disciple who most strongly insisted he would never desert Jesus was (a) John, (b) Matthew, (c) Peter.

4. While Jesus prayed in the Garden, the disciples (a) watched for the soldiers, (b) slept, (c) prayed.

5. Those responsible for the release of Barabbas were (a) the soldiers, (b) the people, (c) the chief priests.

6. The crown of thorns was put on Jesus by (a) Pilate, (b) the Jewish rulers, (c) the soldiers.

7. Christ died at (a) the sixth hour, (b) the ninth hour, (c) the twelfth hour.

8. The parting of Jesus' clothes was the fulfillment of a prophecy in (a) Isaiah, (b) Zechariah, (c) Psalms.

9. The greatest agony the Lord Jesus endured was (a) the physical suffering, (b) the betrayal by Judas, (c) God's turning from Him.

10. The man who asked for the body of Jesus was (a) Zacchaeus, (b) Joseph of Arimathea, (c) Nicodemus.

Turn to page 77 and check your answers.

God's Servant Triumphant

MARK 16

Chapter 16 gives the account of the resurrection and ascension.

1. Who were the first people to go to the tomb?

16:1 _____

2. If the women had really understood what Jesus had taught, would they have gone to the tomb with spices?

16:1 _____

3. On what day was Jesus raised from the dead?

16:2 _____

It is sometimes said that there is no New Testament command for the Lord's Day taking the place of the Mosaic Sabbath. There was no need of words to enact the change for it was legislated into practice by divine action. The resurrection of the world's Savior speaks louder than any words.

4. What question came to mind as the women were approaching the tomb?

16:3-4 _____

5. Had the stone been rolled away to let Jesus out or to let the women see in?

MATTHEW 28:2 _____

6. Who were the witnesses of the resurrection?

16:4 _____

16:5 _____

7. What surprise did the witnesses have?

16:4 _____

8. What had Jesus said about Himself that was proved by the resurrection?

ROMANS 1:4 _____

9. How did the angel prove to the woman that Jesus was risen?

16:6 _____

10. Who was to be given a special message?

16:7 _____

11. Where had Jesus said He would meet His disciples?

16:7; cf. 14:28 _____

12. What did the excited women do?

16:8 _____

13. To whom did they first tell the news?

JOHN 20:2 _____

14. By whom was Jesus seen first?

16:9 _____

15. What background did Mary Madalene have before she followed Jesus?

16:9 _____

16. In what state were Jesus' followers before they heard the news?

16:10 _____

17. What was their reaction to Mary Magdalene's words?

16:11 _____

What becomes of the modern theory that Jesus' disciples had worked themselves up into such a fever of expectation that the wish was father to the thought? The record tells us that they were not in a frame of mind to believe it and did not until they were shown.

18. Who tells the story of what took place between Jesus and the two with whom He walked?

LUKE 24:13-35 _____

19. To whom did Jesus later appear?

16:14 _____

20. What part did the apostles have in the events of the day of resurrection?

16:1-14 _____

21. What Great Commission did the risen Savior give?

16:15 _____

_____

22. How did the disciples respond to the command of Mark 16:15?

16:20 _____

23. What command is linked with a true acceptance of Christ?

16:16 _____

24. What does the outward rite of baptism symbolize?

ROMANS 6:4-5 _____

25. Why were signs necessary before the completion of the written Word?

16:17-20 _____ _____

_____

Remember that Christianity was going forth alone in the hands of a few humble fishermen to grapple with systems that had held sway over the world for centuries.

26. How long was Jesus with His disciples after the resurrection?

ACTS 1:3 _____

27. In what words is the wonderful event of the ascension recorded?

16:19 _____

_____

28. Did the post-resurrection appearance of Jesus have any impact on the disciples?

16:19-20 _____

29. How did Jesus confirm His presence with the disciples after the ascension?

16:20 _____

30. What is Jesus doing for us now at the right hand of God?

HEBREWS 4:14-16; 7:25 _____

check-up time No. 8

You have just studied some important truths about the resurrection of the Lord Jesus. Review your study by rereading the questions and your written answers for lesson 12. If you aren't sure of an answer, reread the Scripture portion given to see if you can find the answer. Then take the following test to see how well you understand the important truths you have studied.

In the right-hand margin write "True" or "False" after each of the following statements.

1. The disciples expected Jesus to rise from the dead. _____

2. Jesus rose from the tomb on the Jewish Sabbath. ___ _____

3. The resurrection is vitally important to Christianity. _____

4. Peter was to be especially notified of what had happened. _____

5. The women immediately told the news to everyone they met. _____

6. Jesus was seen by His mother first. _____

7. Jesus gave His followers work to do. _____

8. Miraculous signs were to be the proof of God's power working in the disciples. _____

9. Jesus was with His disciples for forty days after His resurrection. _____

10. Jesus was taken up into heaven. _____

Turn to page 77 and check your answers.

Suggestions for class use

1. The class teacher may wish to tear this page from each workbook as the answer key is on the reverse side.

2. The teacher should study the lesson first, filling in the blanks in the workbook. He should be prepared to give help to the class on some of the harder places in the lesson. He should also take the self-check tests himself, check his answers with the answer key, and look up any question answered incorrectly.

3. Class sessions can be supplemented by the teacher's giving a talk or leading a discussion on the subject to be studied. The class could then fill in the workbook together as a group, in teams, or individually. If so desired by the teacher, however, this could be done at home. The self-check tests can be done as homework by the class.

4. The self-check tests may be corrected at the beginning of each class session. A brief discussion of the answers can serve as review for the previous lesson.

5. The teacher should motivate and encourage his students. Some public recognition might well be given to class members who successfully complete this course.

answer key
to self-check tests

Be sure to look up any questions you answered incorrectly.

A gives the correct *answer*.

L gives the correct *lesson*.

R *refers* you back to the number of the question in the lesson itself, where the correct answer is to be found.

Mark with an "X" your wrong answers.

	TEST 1			TEST 2			TEST 3			TEST 4		
	A	L	R	A	L	R	A	L	R	A	L	R
1	T	1	3	F	2	2	c	3	2	c	5	3
2	F	1	2	T	2	3	c	3	3	c	5	8
3	T	1	3	T	2	8	a	3	17	a	5	23
4	F	1	9	F	2	20	c	3	27	b	5	27
5	T	1	5	F	2	24	b	3	31	a	5	34
6	F	1	13	T	2	31	a	3	42	b	5	32
7	T	1	19	T	2	36	b	4	6	c	5	33
8	T	1	27	T	2	41	a	4	4	b	5	42
9	T	1	35	T	2	47	c	4	11	c	5	43
10	F	1	39	T	2	50	c	4	23	c	5	39

	TEST 5			TEST 6			TEST 7			TEST 8		
	A	L	R	A	L	R	A	L	R	A	L	R
1	T	6	1	F	8	1	c	10	1	F	12	16
2	F	6	7	F	8	7	a	10	9	F	12	3
3	F	6	9	T	8	11	c	10	17	T	12	8
4	T	6	12	T	9	16	b	10	25	T	12	10
5	T	7	8	F	8	31	c	11	7	F	12	12
6	F	7	17	T	8	36	c	11	12	F	12	14
7	F	7	21	T	9	12	b	11	22	T	12	21
8	T	6	28	T	9	21	c	11	16	T	12	25
9	F	7	27	T	9	18	c	11	24	T	12	26
10	F	7	32	T	9	27	b	11	32	T	12	27

How well did you do?

0-1 wrong answers—excellent work

2-3 wrong answers—review errors carefully

4 or more wrong answers—restudy the lesson before going on to the next one

Moody Press, a ministry of the Moody Bible Institute, is designed for education, evangelization, and edification. If we may assist you in knowing more about Christ and the Christian life, please write us without obligation: Moody Press, c/o MLM, Chicago, Illnois 60610.